COUNTRY LIVING

M A G A Z I N E

COUNTRY
BEARS

EBURY PRESS LONDON

First published in Great Britain in 1991 by Ebury Press
an imprint of the Random Century Group
Random Century House
20 Vauxhall Bridge Road
London SWIV 2SA

Published by arrangement with Hearst Books, an affiliate of William Morrow
and Company, Inc., 1350 Avenue of the Americas, New York, N.Y. 10019.

A catalogue record for this book is available from the British Library.

ISBN 0 09 175195 0

Country Living Staff USA
Rachel Newman, Editor
Bo Niles, Senior Editor

Designed by Barbara Scott—Goodman
Edited by Suni Prete
Produced by Smallwood and Stewart, Inc., New York City

CONTENTS:

I must have been a rebel from an early age because when my parents took me to the toy department of a large London store and asked me to choose from a selection of golden yellow and brown teddy bears, I chose a blue one. Bitterly disappointed that I had not bonded with any of their favourites, they took me and "Richard" home, defiant but happy. I named him Richard after my imaginary, and until then, invisible soulmate and playmate. In my blue bear I had recognised his physical manifestation. He is still with me 36 years later, a little paler and flatter —my mother insisted he was washed and mangled dry regularly. But he remained loyal to me where some humans have not; listened to my troubles when my friends have tired; and given me solace when I needed it. I could never feel the same way about a doll—you just can't cuddle a doll like you can a bear. I know I am not alone in my affection for the teddy bear as this delightful collection by Bo Niles and Rachel Newman bears out!

Francine Lawrence
Editor, *Country Living Magazine*

ertain experiences are common to all children and one of the more endearing is the attachment to a teddy bear. There probably isn't one among us who can't remember the comforting effect of cuddling up to a teddy bear at night. The rugged, eyeless, little creatures we see at auctions and antiques shops today are a testament to the power they have had, and continue to have, over us. You really don't have to be young to find a friend in a teddy bear.

Rachel Newman
Country Living, USA

dozen little bears inhabit our home—hardly enough to constitute a collection, but loving enough to be family to my husband, sons and myself. Terrycloth Ed, the first bear, I sewed together as we awaited the arrival of our first son. Harold, a traditional Steiff, joined us shortly after. A koala (Kenny) and three pandas (Mo, Molly, and Malone) followed Harold: Technically they aren't really bears, but they do have the same affectionate appeal. (A koala is a marsupial and the panda is a relative of the raccoon.) Then Harry and Carrie moved in, and then Mary, the bear with the bandaged paw. And our little family is still growing!

Teddy bears, with their plush, huggable bodies and amiable expressions, seem to possess an endearing quality of listening without judging. They bring out the best in us by fostering feelings of comfort, trust and love. Teddies, with their soothing faces, help the young and the old—and those somewhere in between—get through difficult times of sickness and need. No wonder that facial expression is the most sought-after quality in a teddy, for children and collectors alike.

For the collector or arctophile ("arcto" from the Greek word for bear), bear collecting is more than a hobby; it's a passion. Teddy bear clubs and organizations abound. Worldwide, thousands of shops sell teddy bears exclusively, and there are several devoted to the bear phenomenon.

COUNTRY LIVING magazine has long celebrated bears; let the celebration continue!

Bo Niles

THE BEAR FACTS
The History of the Teddy Bear

Teddy as toy. Teddy as playmate. Teddy as collectible. Teddy bears are an integral part of our culture and so well loved that they are synonymous with warmth, humour, and affection. So many of us—adults and children alike—own at least one teddy that it's difficult to believe that there haven't always been teddy bears to play with and share secrets with.

•

The teddy's origins, although certainly not shrouded in the mists of time, have been obscured by conflict and counterclaim. The Americans take a proprietary interest: the most popular tale centres on President Theodore—Teddy—Roosevelt. The British, however, contend that King Edward VII—Ted—who enjoyed viewing the bears at London Zoo, was actually responsible for the teddy bear's name. It is generally agreed that the toy bear was born in the first few years of the twentieth century.

In the American version, President Roosevelt was on a fact-finding trip to Mississippi over the causes of a border dispute with Louisiana when he was invited on a bear hunt. An ardent hunter all his life, he had never bagged a bear. Bears were considered terrifying predators at the time, worthy of the kill. Roosevelt's companions, spying an exhausted older bear near a watering hole, caught it easily and tied it to a tree. Roosevelt was summoned to make the fatal shot. In this unfair and unsportsmanlike set-up, the president refused to shoot.

•

Clifford Berryman, a cartoonist for the *Washington Post*, drew parallels between Roosevelt's act and the political feud between Mississippi and Louisiana. His cartoon of Roosevelt sparing the bear was captioned "Drawing the Line in Mississippi;" it called national attention to the hunting incident and, of course, to the sorrowful captive bear.

In Brooklyn, New York, Morris and Rose Michtom, recent immigrants from Russia, were inspired by the cartoon to create a special window display for their novelty shop. To entice passersby, Rose stitched up two bears of furry brown mohair and placed them alongside a copy of the cartoon. Orders flooded the shop, and Morris sent one of Rose's creations to the president, asking for permission to call his popular new toys "Teddy's Bears." Roosevelt complied.

The Michtoms continued to make bears and eventually formed the very successful Ideal Toy Company. Today one of the original Ideal teddy bears from 1903 is on exhibit at the Smithsonian Institution in Washington, D.C.

•

Meanwhile, in Germany, Margarete Steiff, confined to a wheelchair as a result of childhood polio, turned to sewing to earn her living. One of her earliest creations, an elephant-shaped

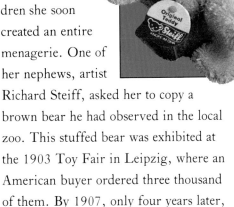

pincushion, became so popular among the local children she soon created an entire menagerie. One of her nephews, artist Richard Steiff, asked her to copy a brown bear he had observed in the local zoo. This stuffed bear was exhibited at the 1903 Toy Fair in Leipzig, where an American buyer ordered three thousand of them. By 1907, only four years later, the Steiff company had manufactured almost a million bears.

•

The story, perhaps apocryphally, runs full circle. It is said that several of these charming bears were presented to the Roosevelt family as decorations for the wedding reception of their daughter Alice. In fact, Roosevelt gleefully wore the label of bear lover as a useful political ploy. Buttons and cartoons depicted him with a supportive bear, sometimes holding a banner extolling

"Four Years More of Theodore." Legend has it that he briefly kept a pair of bear cubs at the White House to entertain his children before donating them to New York City's Bronx Zoo, where they were introduced to the public as "Teddy's Bears."

•

In these early days of color printing, teddy bear postcards, paper dolls, and advertising on cereal and Cracker Jack boxes combined with Roosevelt memorabilia to stoke the mania for this newfangled toy. Teddy's bears even began to sport Rough Rider outfits. Paul Piper, under the pen name of Seymour Eaton, wrote a quartet of childrens' books entitled *The Roosevelt Bears.* He named his characters Teddy-B and Teddy-G. The first book appeared just before Christmas in 1906. The publication of these books standardized the use of "teddy bear".

Teddies are among the well-worn and loved animals of these cupboard menageries.

▄▄▄▄▄▄▄▄▄▄▄▄▄▄▄▄▄▄▄▄▄▄▄▄▄▄

Bear, Bear, don't go away

To come again some other
day

I will love you if you stay

I will love you any way.

"Early 20th Century Greeting Card"

▄▄▄▄▄▄▄▄▄▄▄▄▄▄▄▄▄▄▄▄▄▄▄▄▄▄

This elder bearsman *by Steiff sports his numerous medals from past heroic feats.*

*Nearly ninety,
Stuffy dons his
newspaper cap—
dated April 11,
1933—with
pride.*

They talked of things

both small and great,

some long forgotten,

some up-to-date;

They laughed at jokes

and spilled their tea

and made a muss

like you and me.

from *The Roosevelt Bears Abroad*
by Seymour Eaton

ANTIQUE BEARS

The teddy bear is a popular collectible that abides by no rules. Teddies are not even unique items: the earliest teddies, predating 1910, numbered in the millions. Still, because of their innate fragility, and because so many have been lost to hug-fostered deterioration, the value of old teddy bears has escalated significantly. Ardent collectors need not panic, however. Many wonderful bears can still be found—if you hunt a little—for a steal!

According to precise definition, a collectible becomes an antique when it reaches the age of one hundred; by all accounts, then, the teddy bear will finally become an "antique" in the year 2003! Most seasoned bear hunters, however, consider teddies made prior to 1940 antiques.

•

Although the teddy bear as a cuddly toy and playmate for children dates from 1903, bear imagery existed long before that time. In the 1880s, for example, seltzer companies and piano manufacturers used bear caricatures in their advertisements. In the mid-1800s, ferocious-looking mechanical and musical bears were popular adult toys. Bears have inspired legend and myth in many cultures and have even been worshipped as deities in some.

As a stuffed toy, the teddy was repeatedly copied. The Steiff firm, under the guidance of Margarete and her nephews, developed bears in a variety of shapes and sizes, all of which enjoyed enormous popularity. Richard Steiff's vision of a fully jointed, mohair-covered bear with a squeezable body became the standard that virtually every other manufacturer emulated.

•

Collecting

Many collectors find that precisely dating a bear can be difficult. Not only were bears produced in great volume over the years, but some manufacturers would meticulously copy earlier, successful bears if they thought those models would still sell well. In fact some reproductions can have enormous value if they have been well executed.

Today prized early bears fetch high prices at auctions. The highest paid to date for a teddy was £55,000 for a bear auctioned at Sotheby's in London in 1989.

•

When you buy a bear, be sure to retain

the purchase receipt plus any tags or other identifying information that accompanies your bear. Ask the salesperson to give you as much written information on your bear as possible. You will want to know the age—even an approximate age will help—and you should ascertain where it came from or was found.

Photograph your bear—front, side and back—as a visual record, especially for insurance purposes. Label each photograph with the name and the value of the bear. Keep the photographs and the written provenance you have compiled. This "dossier" will prove invaluable if you anticipate any future repairs or cleaning for your bear.

Some Characteristics of Early Collectible Antique Teddy Bears

* Covering is made of long or short mohair; the best bears boast fur in good or mint condition, with few, if any, worn patches.
* Stuffing is excelsior, which is created from wood shavings, or straw, and fills the bear firmly.
* Face has original shoe-button eyes and an elongated snout with an embroidered nose and mouth.
* Back has a hump between the shoulders.
* Body is fully jointed, with rather heavy legs and very large, goofy-looking feet, long narrow arms reaching to the knees, and elongated paws with felt pads and embroidered claws.
* If bear is a Steiff, it has a signature "Knopf in Ohr" or "Button in Ear;" a bear with a blank button predates 1907.
* A bear with a center seam on the head is very rare, as are bears with open mouths, especially with teeth.

T he world has room to make a bear feel free;
The universe seems cramped to you and me. . . .

from "The Bear"
by Robert Frost

The elongated snout with its embroidered nose and the over-sized paws attest to the early manufacture of this bear.

Unusual antique bears inhabit this cupboard: a miniature bear, a rare open-mouthed bear,
and a bear with red ears.

Drawing perhaps on their reputations for facial excellence, a trio of teddies seems mildly bewildered by a group of faceless rag dolls.

TODAY'S BEARS

Today's teddy bears can be divided into three categories. The most common, mass-produced bears are toys manufactured by companies that specialize in making stuffed animals. Designer bears are developed by artists and craftspeople to be manufactured by smaller speciality companies. Artist bears, which are classified as either one-of-a-kind, open-edition, or limited-edition collectibles, are originated by artists who conceive, design, and construct the bears according to their imagination and talent; these teddies are named, signed, and numbered, which is a testament to their individuality.

The publication of *The Teddy Bear Book* by Peter Bull in 1970 heralded a renaissance of interest in the teddy bear which was previously considered merely a plaything. Suddenly thousands of secret bear lovers emerged, thus creating a new market for collectible bears. Artist bears gratified those who longed to own a special bear but did not want an antique, which might already be, literally, "loved to death."

●

Teddy bear historians trace the trend in artist bears to 1980 and the publication of an influential book, *The Teddy Bear Catalog* by Alan and Peggy Bialosky. The book stimulated craftspeople to turn to making bears as an outlet for their skills and artistry. Some of the earliest artists, in fact, developed bears with their prior expertise in doll-making; many bears from the early 1980s exhibited doll-like features, notably porcelain faces and costuming.

Other artists, looking for the perfect toy for a newborn child, considered bears. They decided to make their own, and in doing so, discovered a craft they could happily do at home while their children were growing up. In some families, the children grew to appreciate their parents' handiwork so much, they also turned to creating and making bears.

●

As the interest in their bears grew, many artists began to convene at newly organized teddy bear fairs and rallies around the country where their bears could be shown and sold. Today there are dozens of teddy bear rallies nationwide, and the phenomenon of artist bears shows no sign of slowing down.

●

A teddy bear artist, by definition and inference, makes only a certain number of bears in a year. The one-of-a-kind bear may be designed according to the artist's whim or fancy, or in response to a particular commission from a collector or organization. Limited-edition bears are conceived and produced in a predetermined quantity. Open edition applies to a particularly popular bear that the artist keeps in continuous production, perhaps over several years, to meet an ongoing demand.

●

Artist bears are always made from specially created patterns that the artist devises, never from commercial patterns. The originality of the concept and design sets the tone of the project, and sets the artist apart from the commercial manufacturer who produces as many bears as toy and department stores will order.

●

A bear can take anywhere from a few hours to a full day to complete, and even longer if it is elaborately costumed. Most artists experiment with an idea by trying out several versions of a particular bear until it turns out just right. Artists create their own patterns, often freehand, and then transfer them onto a durable kraft paper or cardboard. The patterns are then outlined in multiple sets onto fabric such as plush or velvet, so that specific parts of the bear can be sewn in an efficient assembly-line manner; for instance, all of the legs are sewn and then all of the arms, and so on. Joints are inserted at the shoulder, neck, and hip. Last to be assembled is typically the head. Before the head is stuffed, the artist sews on the safety-lock eyes and embroiders the mouth and nose.

●

Teddy bear artists always pay particular attention to creating captivating facial expressions for their bears, ones which will express the "soul" of the bear. Indeed, many artists today ascribe mystical qualities to each of their bears and enjoy knowing that a bear will become a "special friend" to a collector.

A recently hand-crafted teddy bear casts an innocent gaze at his many admirers.

This teddy, decked out in majestic regalia and armed with a book of fairy-tales, is ready to battle a long winter's night.

Goldilocks and the Three Bears (above), a skydiving bear (left), and an assortment of bears (opposite), including three fashioned of twigs, are literary and humorous variations on the traditional teddy.

If you go down in the
woods today

You'd better not go alone

It's lovely down in the
woods today

But safer to stay
at home

For ev'ry Bear
that ever there was

Will gather there
for certain because

Today's the day the
Teddy Bears
have their Picnic

Teddy Bears' Picnic
lyrics by Jimmy Kennedy

*Designed with character, these colorful
and amusing bears add charm to their
respective environments.*

There was an
Old Person of Ware,

Who rode on the back
of a Bear;

When they ask'd,
"Does it trot?"

He said, "certainly not!"

He's a Moppsikon
Floppsikon Bear!"

Edward Lear

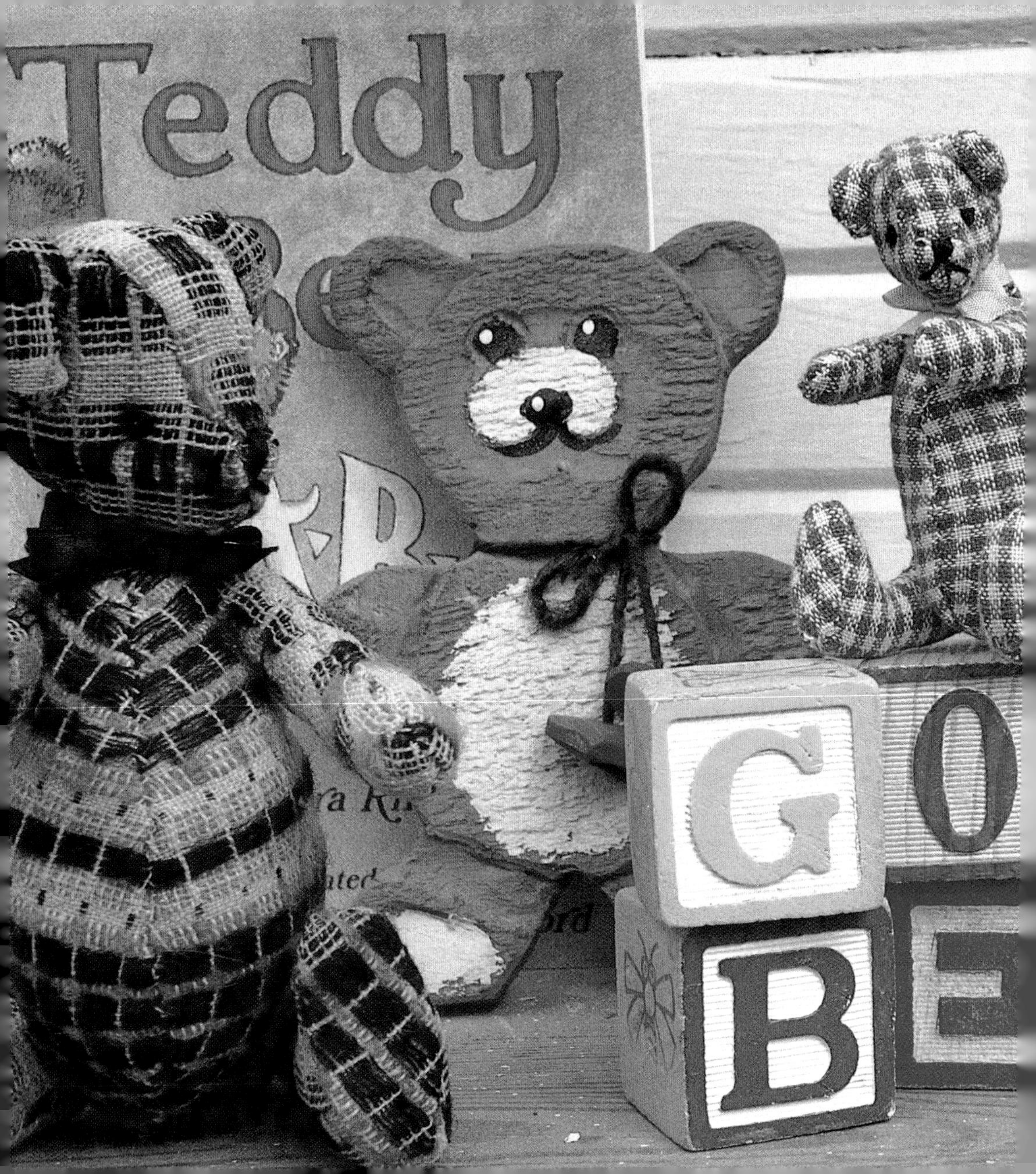
Teddy
G
O
B

TEDDY BEAR CARE

The teddy bear subsists on a healthy diet of affection, cuddling, and rugged hugging. But the bear's very sustenance can be the cause of certain treatable ailments such as bald spots, stains, exhausted stuffing, and missing shoe buttons and paws. In fact, the older your teddy is, the more likely he bears one or two of these tokens of love.

Teddies made since the 1950s, by law, have been crafted of materials that are safe for children and are cleanable. Antique teddies, and limited-edition or collectible teddies, however, still require special care because of the delicate construction.

Treating Your Bear

An antique bear may suffer internal as well as external damage. The stuffing in older bears can eventually decay into a fine powder, a condition known as dry rot. To avoid this, fumigate your bear before repairing and cleaning it. First wrap it in a plastic bag—to protect its fragile fur. Then place the bear in an airtight container with a handful of mothballs. Leave it in the container for four days before airing it out.

●

A damaged antique bear may also need to have its stuffing revived or replenished. You can supplement depleted stuffing with excelsior salvaged from other stuffed animals damaged beyond repair, or you can add new material. The best new stuffing is easily created from cut-up hosiery that has had the elastic bands removed. Use the blunt end of a crochet hook to insert the hosiery fragments, bit by bit, between the stitches of the exposed seams where

the stuffing seems most exhausted. Do not pack the new stuffing too tightly, since this may cause the bear's fragile seams to split open.

●

When repairing a seam or rip, try to use strong cotton thread in a shade that matches your bear's fur, so that the stitches will be less visible. Synthetic thread can be used, of course, but it tends to look slightly shiny against fur and cloth.

•

If the rip is narrow, gently pull the two sides of the tear together and pin them with dressmaker's pins. Use a herringbone stitch across the opening. Do not tug at the thread too tightly; this may cause the surrounding fabric to fray and could also create a ridge along the ripped area. Poke any exposed stuffing back into the bear as you sew. If the opening or hole is wide and the edges of the tear cannot be pulled together, you may have to reinforce the entire damaged area with bolder darning stitches.

•

Some collectors counsel against replacing limbs or eyes, to preserve the history of the bear's life. Others find missing parts tragic and intolerable. If you are of the latter school of thought, keep a selection of replacement eyes—

found in a craft shop—or antique shoe buttons on hand.

•

New limbs can be created from old, matching materials. A counterfeit limb can be "camouflaged" by dressing the damaged bear in a long-sleeved coat or in trousers.

•

Cleaning Your Antique Teddy Bear
Because most antique teddies are collected not as toys but for display, they typically only need periodic cleaning to maintain their surface luster and softness. Surface cleaning can be easily accomplished with a vacuum adjusted at the gentlest setting. If your bear has any dirty spots, first sprinkle a teaspoon or so of cornmeal directly on the soiled area. Leave the cornmeal on the stain for twenty-four hours, then vacuum your bear.

•

When you vacuum, you'll want to protect your bear's fragile fur— especially mohair—from shedding.

Tape two layers of cheesecloth or hosiery over the nozzle of the vacuum to cushion the force of the suction. You should not allow the nozzle to come into direct contact with the fur. Vacuum the bear's surface in small but overlapping circles, first clockwise and then counterclockwise, to ensure that you remove all the accumulated dust.

●

Bathing Your New Collectible Bear
An artist or limited-edition bear cannot be washed or dried in laundry machines. Most collectors, in fact, never wash their bears, no matter how dirty they may be. Others, however, believe an occasional sponge-and-brush bath will actually enhance both the appearance and the value of a beloved teddy.

●

Before attempting to wash your bear, test a concealed spot, such as an armpit, to see if washing will cause any shedding, staining , or fading to the bear's coat.

Clean your bear only with soapsuds, since soapy liquid can saturate and damage the bear's coat and stuffing. Gather some suds, made from mild detergent, onto a long-handled, soft-bristled brush or a toothbrush. Gently stroke the suds into the fur of the bear's coat in small, clockwise circles. Be sure to work on a very small portion of the bear at a time. Work across the front of the bear first, then the back, the head, and each limb. Gently wipe the suds off with a damp washcloth, working in counterclockwise circles. Continue the suds-rinsing procedure, portion by portion, until the bear is fully clean.

●

You can either set your bear outside to dry or use a hand-held hair dryer adjusted to the lowest heat setting. If you set your bear outside, do not leave it in the sunlight too long; its fur may fade or discolor. Once the bear is dry, fluff up its fur with a clean, soft-bristled toothbrush or a fine-toothed comb.

A couple of well-groomed and dressed-up bears are on display.

Whether a bear is stored or displayed, a cool, dry environment is best, and will help deter future damage. If you do plan to store your bear, wrap it loosely in a light-colored cotton pillowcase or towel and place it on a shelf in a dark, well-ventilated closet. Never store your bear in a plastic bag; like any item made of fabric, it requires air to prevent mildew. Mothballs will also damage a bear, especially an old one made of natural fibers and stuffing. To ward off moths place a cedar block or two, also wrapped in cotton cloth, in the closet.

Sit still as mice on this occasion

And listen to the Bears' Invasion

Of Sicily, a long, long while

Ago when beasts were good, men vile.

from *The Bears' famous Invasion of Sicily*
by Dino Buzzati

TEDDY BEAR DISPLAY

Teddy bears add a warm country atmosphere and touch of humor to any room. So why not rescue those old bears tucked away in the closet or attic and display them with pride. Group teddies on hatboxes and bookshelves and in baskets in the kitchen, or perhaps among a prized stoneware collection in an antique cupboard. Surround them with other cherished childhood toys on a dresser or nightstand; move them periodically from one setting to another. Whether nestled on a quilt, napping on a guest bed, or sunning on the window sill, teddy bears exude charm.

Every teddy is a show-off at heart and desires more than anything to be in full view of an affectionate, even adoring, public. Because a teddy's disposition is sociable, he prefers not to be alienated from other bears. The hospitable teddy would rather fraternize with his cohorts than be isolated. But teddies, in the unfortunate absence of other bears, would choose to mingle with other toys and collectibles than be confined to a lonely part of the house.

•

Most bears, especially antique teddies, are fully jointed and can be positioned with ease and flexibility. The only necessity for a teddy's comfort and for his longevity is keeping him away from dirt, grease, and moisture.

•

If your bears are unclad, dress them up and create your own character bears. Scraps of fabric found around the house can be easily and stylishly transformed into teddy attire. A plaid ribbon tied around your bear will instantly put him in the holiday spirit. A pair of old sun glasses and a Hawaiian-print fabric will have him ready for the beach in no time. Lace and flowers and a little satin can turn your plain teddy into a fuzzy angel.

•

The varied and individual personalities of an assembly of bears may prompt idiosyncratic staging. A pair of well-loved teddies can lead a wedding procession across a bureau, for instance. Or you might invite a tribe of relatives on an outing in an antique roadster. Costumed and character bears enjoy the context of a backdrop to enhance their attire. Create a forest for Winnie-the-Pooh, a palace for your crowned bear and his jesters, or a

sleigh-ride setting for those bears in thick winter sweaters.

•

Of course, the most felicitous display is a spontaneous gesture of love or a flight of fancy. The nightly ritual of a teddy tucked in the crook of a sleeping child's elbow or a bear snuggled up in an armchair between grandchild and grandparent remind us that the teddy was born as a toy and grew into a collectible with the passage of time. Teddies are displayed so that they will be cherished by all who come in contact with them.

While a lone bear keeps watch in a hutch of rooster-print stoneware (right), a group of teddies occupies the second story of a toy collector's cupboard (opposite).

Place miniature calico bears in a twig basket (below) and teddies with dolls in an antique wagon (opposite) to create a rustic atmosphere.

Ushering in springtime festivities, this teddy attempts an all-too-familiar disguise.

*A very proper bear
requires fine china
and frills when
taking her tea.*

From California coastal cool (left) to Southern reserve (opposite), these bears are prepared for a long, hot summer.

An Amish bear (left) and traditionally attired teddies in New England (opposite) enjoy the filtered rays and crisp, cool air of autumn.

Ready, set, snow! Bundled up and determined to have fun, a young trio takes to sleigh-riding during the cold winter months.

Y is for Yuletide

The grown people's name

For the time

when my Teddy

From Santa Claus came.

Anonymous

For decades the little teddy bear has been making an appearance during the holiday season, spreading warmth and cheer.

Blackbeard

Magical and mythical apparel turns everyday bears into wizards, fairies, pirates and more!

Breathing at my side, that heavy animal,

That heavy bear who sleeps with me,

Howls in his sleep for a world of sugar . . .

from "The Heavy Bear Who Goes With Me"
by Delmore Schwartz

A miniature bear and his miniature, quilt-covered bed.

A bigger bear on his own people-sized, quilt-covered bed.

Teddy bear, teddy bear, turn around.

Teddy bear, teddy bear, touch the ground.

Teddy bear, teddy bear, switch off the light.

Teddy bear, teddy bear, say "Good Night."

Anonymous

TEDDY BEAR RESOURCE GUIDE
Listed below is a selection of events, magazines, manufacturers and professionals in the growing world of teddy bears.

BEAR EVENTS:

For information on smaller and local events check with the magazines listed below.

The British Teddy Bear
Festival
Kensington Town Hall
London W8
For more information
write to:
Hugglets
PO Box 290
Brighton
BN2 1DR
*Every August Bank Holiday.
Over 100 exhibitors with
5,000 teddy bears for sale, plus
repairs, valuations and talks.*

London Toy Convention
Ramada Inn West London
Lillie Rd
London SW6
For more information
write to:
Jack's Wall
Littlehempston

Totnes, Devon
TQ9 6LY
*Held twice a year in London
and always includes teddy bears.*

London International
Antiques Dolls, Toys,
Miniatures & Teddy Bear
Fair
Kensington Town Hall
London W8
For more information
write to:
PO Box 734
Forest Hill
London SE22 8DR
*Held five times every year and
includes teddy bears amongst
many wonderful antique toys.*

The Winter BearFest
Civic Hall, Rother Street
Stratford-upon-Avon
For more information
write to:
Hugglets, PO Box 290
Brighton
BN2 1DR

*Early February each year.
Thousands of bears, plus
repairs, valuations and
displays.*

MAGAZINES:

Hugglets Teddy Bear
Magazine
PO Box 290
Brighton BN2 1DR
*Published four times a year.
News, bear history, features,
fair dates.*

Teddy Bear Times
Ashdown Publishing
104 High Street
Steyning
West Sussex BN4 3RD
Published four times a year.

UK Teddy Bear Guide
PO Box 290
Brighton BN2 1DR
*Directory of all teddy businesses
in the United Kingdom.*

TEDDY BEAR PROFESSIONALS

Sue Pearson
13½ Prince Albert Street
The Lanes, Brighton
East Sussex BN1 1HE
*Buyer and seller of antique
teddy bears, free valuations.
Teddy bear and doll hospital.*

Pam Hebbs
5 The Annexe
Camden Passage
Islington, London N1
*Old teddies bought and sold.
Steiff animals always in stock.
Exclusive lines.*

Teddy Bears of Witney
99 High Street
Witney
Oxfordshire OX8 6LY
*Excellent selection of old and
new bears. Replica Steiffs
available.*

Asquiths Teddy Bear Shops
10 George V Place
Thames Avenue
Windsor
Berkshire SL4 1QP
*The first exclusively teddy bear
shop in England.*

Also at:
2-4 New Street
Henley-on-Thames
Oxfordshire RG9 2BT

*Also stocks famous 'Henley
Bear' in regatta costume*
and
33 High Street
Eton
Berkshire SL4 6AX
*The largest shop and packed
with bears from all over the
world.*

MANUFACTURERS AND SUPPLIERS

Merrythought
Ironbridge
Telford
Shropshire
TF8 7NJ
Founded in 1930, this leading teddy bear manufacturer is producing a new range of traditional collectables this year.

Dean's Company
Pontnewynydd Industrial Estate
Pontypool
Gwent
NP4 6YY
Suppliers of traditional jointed bears as well as many others.

Canterbury Bears
The Old Coach House
Court Hill
Littlebourne
Canterbury
CT3 1TY
Teddy bear specialists, who produce traditional jointed bears made in wool, mohair and alpaca.

Recollect Studios
Dept TBG
The Old School

London Road
Sayers Common
West Sussex
BN6 9HX
Mohair fabric and all bear-making supplies, including growls, glass eyes, stuffing, joints, nose thread, teddy bear books. Also run teaching programmes on teddy bear making.

Gabrielle Designs
The Bear Garden

Great North Road
Adwick-le-Street
Doncaster
South Yorkshire
DN6 7EJ
The sole manufacturer of the famous Paddington Bear as well as other charming teddies.

TEDDY BEAR GROUPS, ATTRACTIONS & MISCELLANY

British Teddy Bear Association
Membership Enquiries:

PO Box 290
Brighton BN2 1DR
Newsletter called 'Bearings'.

Good Bears of the World
Membership enquiries:
c/o Jill Skinner
43 Merley Drive, Highcliffe
Christchurch
Dorset BH23 5BW
Charity supplying teddies to those in need.

The Bear Museum
38 Dragon Street
Petersfield
Hampshire GU31 4JJ
Restorations, museum, replicas, antique dolls. Free entry.

The Teddy Bear Museum
19 Greenhill Street
Stratford-upon-Avon
Warwickshire CV37 6LF
Award winning museum, featuring hundreds of famous bears.

The Cotswold Teddy Bear Museum
76 High Street
Broadway
Cotswolds
Worcestershire WR12 7AJ
Recently opened museum for teddies.

Eversley Bears Guest House
37 Grove Road
Stratford-upon-Avon
Warwickshire CU37 6PB
Family-run guest house which is the home of a large collection of bears.

With thanks to the UK Teddy Bear Guide for information supplied.

ACKNOWLEDGMENTS

Page 14, Copyright 1903 by Raphael Tuck and Sons Co. Ltd., New York.

Page 19, from *The Roosevelt Bears Abroad*, "The Bears Meet the King" Seymour Eaton, No. V., © 1907, *The Sunday Oregonian*, March 3, 1907.

Page 24, from *The Poetry of Robert Frost* edited by Edward Connery Lathem. Copyright 1928, © 1969 by Holt Rinehart and Winston. Copyright © 1956 by Robert Frost. Reprinted with permission of Henry Holt and Company, Inc.

Page 40, "Teddy Bears' Picnic," lyrics by Jimmy Kennedy, music by J.E. Bratton, © 1907.

Page 55, from *The Bears' famous Invasion of Sicily* by Dino Buzzati, translated by Frances Lobb, © 1947 by Rizzoli for Pantheon Books, Inc.

Page 83, from *Selected Poems: Summer Knowledge* by Delmore Schwartz. Copyright © 1959 by Delmore Schwartz. Reprinted with permission of New Directions Publishing Corporation. World rights.

Pages 62–63, 68–69, 78–79 and left photo on 90: Mohair-covered bears by Debra Malik Demosthenes.

Pages 42–43, 46–47: jointed bears from recycled coats and scrap-bag fabric by Charlene O'Neill and Beth Cooper.

BIBLIOGRAPHY

Bialosky, Peggy and Alan *The Teddy Bear Catalog* Workman Publishing Co., Inc., 1984, 224 pp.

Bull, Peter *The Teddy Bear Book* Random House, Inc., 1970, 207 pp.

Hillier, Mary *Teddy Bears: A Celebration* Beaufort Books Publishers, 1985, 96 pp.

Hutchings, Margaret *Teddy Bears and How to Make Them* Dover Publications, Inc., 1977, 283 pp. (This is the American edition of the British original *Book of the Teddy Bear*, Mills and Boon, 1964.)

Mullins, Linda *Teddy Bears Past & Present: A Collector's Identification Guide* Hobby House Press, Inc., 1986, 304 pp.

Picot, Genevieve and Gerard *Bears* Harmony Books, 1988, 120 pp.

Schoonmaker, Patricia *Collector's History of the Teddy Bear* Hobby House Press, Inc., 1981, 312 pp.

Volpp, Rosemary and Paul; Harrison, Donna; Ayers, Dottie *Teddy Bear Artist's Annual* Hobby House Press, Inc., 1989, 128 pp.

Waugh, Carol-Lynn Rössel
Teddy Bear Artists: Romance of Making & Collecting Teddy Bears
Hobby House Press, Inc., 1984, 208 pp.

PHOTOGRAPHY CREDITS

Front and Back
Cover	Paul Kopelow
2	Paul Kopelow
4–5	André Gillardin
8–9	Keith Scott Morton
11	Keith Scott Morton
12	André Gillardin
13	Jessie Walker
14–15	André Gillardin
16	Paul Kopelow
17	Keith Scott Morton
18	Jessie Walker
20–21	Jessie Walker
23	Jessie Walker
24	Lynn Karlin
25	Jessie Walker
26	Jessie Walker
27	Jon Elliott
28–29	Keith Scott Morton
30–31	Jessie Walker
34	Keith Scott Morton
35	Jon Elliott
36	Paul Kopelow
37	Jessie Walker
38–39	Keith Scott Morton
40–41	Keith Scott Morton
42	Jon Elliott (upper left), Jessie Walker (lower left and upper right)
43	Jon Elliott (upper left and upper right), Keith Scott Morton (lower right)
44–45	Jessie Walker
46–47	Paul Kopelow
48–49	Jessie Walker
50	Paul Kopelow
53	Paul Kopelow
54	Ralph Bogertman
55	Jessie Walker (top), James Levin (bottom)
56–57	Paul Kopelow
58–59	Jessie Walker
60	Jon Elliott
61	Jessie Walker
62	Al Teufen
63	André Gillardin
64	Keith Scott Morton
65	Keith Scott Morton
66	Jessie Walker
67	Jessie Walker
68	Paul Kopelow
69	Keith Scott Morton
70	Jessie Walker
71	Keith Scott Morton
72–73	Jessie Walker
74	Jessie Walker
75	Jon Elliott
76	Keith Scott Morton (top left), Jessie Walker (right), Jon Elliott (bottom left)
77	Jon Elliott
78–79	Jessie Walker
80	Paul Kopelow
81	Jessie Walker (top left), Paul Kopelow (bottom left and right)
82–83	Jon Elliott
84	Ralph Bogertman
85	James Levin
86–87	Al Teufen
88	Paul Kopelow
89	Rick Patrick
91	Jon Elliott
92	Keith Scott Morton
93	Al Teufen
96	Paul Kopelow